KING OF THE CASTLE

KING OF THE CASTLE

The Way Out for Christian Men with Addictions

Peter Jones

First published by Independent Publishing Network 2021

Copyright © 2021 by Peter Jones

ISBN 978-1-80049-910-2

Edited by Janet Schwind

First edition

ENDORSEMENTS

For too long the plague of addiction in the church has prevented men from embracing their God-given significance and pursuing all that the Lord has for them. Peter's writings are practical, inspired and a gift to us all. *King of the Castle* is a prophetic work for our time. Read this and significant things will follow.

Rev. Dave Larlee | Priest, Pitboss. Dallas, Texas

* * *

This book is dynamite. Read it, apply it, and walk in the freedom Jesus won for us.

Simon Ponsonby | Pastor of Theology, St. Aldates Church, Oxford UK

* * *

Seriously guys, this is a "must read"! If I can be even stronger, find a close friend or a group of friends, and do this journey with them. You'll so value their support and encouragement, and you will be free! Peter has been ruthlessly honest about himself on his journey from addiction to freedom: I know this will be a life-saver for you!

Gordon Hickson | Author, Harnessed for Adventure

It is with enthusiasm and honour that I commend this book to you. Peter Jones is the real deal. He is a passionate, humble, visionary leader of people. Peter has done his work in this area and is emerging with a freedom, a story to tell and some real wisdom to impart. This book is the real deal too, uncomfortable and practical in all the right ways. Engaging with the truths within will not only be worthwhile but might be life-changing.

Karl Martin | Founder, Arable

* * *

I cannot urge you strongly enough to read this book. The images and revelations are so powerful, in many places I had to stop and catch my breath. This book will change the way I pray, and as a Catholic, the book reinforces the role and power of the sacraments in my life. Amazing!

Ron Huntley | Author, Unlocking Your Parish

* * *

Peter is a man worth listening to with a vital message for our time. If you are like me, regularly looking for voices further down the road who are filled with integrity, wisdom, and helpful insight, you'll quickly recognize that you've found it in Peter and what he shares in *King of the Castle*.

Craig Springer | Executive Director, Alpha USA, Author, How to Follow Jesus and How to Revive Evangelism

CONTENTS

DEDICATION

To you.
Pick up your sword one more time.

INTRODUCTION

I WANT TO TALK TO you about addiction. We tend to treat addiction as if it were an illness, a frustrating, damaging affliction. We treat it psychologically with counselling and cognitive therapies, with medication to chemically numb its effects, and sociologically with various programs. All of these can be helpful at the right time. However, I am convinced that unless we deal with the root causes and understand the mechanisms involved in addiction, we will be left fighting symptoms without finding a real solution.

I am a Christian. I see things from a spiritual perspective. I believe in spiritual forces that are working for us and against us, and have been all our lives. I believe we are made in God's image, by a loving Father, for love. I believe we each have a destiny, both while we are here on earth and throughout eternity. I have also come to realize addiction is not just something that happens to some of us, but it is a strategy of the forces working against us to keep us from our destinies. The very fact that you have an addiction may be a sign that God has a higher calling for you and a plan for your life that the enemy is trying to derail.

I do not speak from an academic standpoint. During my life I have been addicted for various lengths of time—and to varying degrees—to nicotine, pornography, alcohol, marijuana, and cocaine. But there have been more subtle addictions. Allowing fear or worry to rule our lives can be just as limiting as a physical or psychological addiction. For me, this had started by the time I was 14 years old, and I struggled, sometimes for years, to free myself of these addictions. I faced failure countless times. There have been seasons when addiction completely dominated my life and my behavior revolved around the subject of the addiction. I remember in Paris one morning, at the age of 18, taking cocaine before breakfast.. I knew then that I was in trouble. But at the same time, I knew I had a calling on my life; I just didn't know what it was.

Over the last 14 years I have also worked in prisons where many of the men and women have serious addiction issues. And I have seen addiction operating in my friends and family, many of them Christians.

I didn't become a Christian until I was 27 years old. When I gave my life to God, I stopped all these destructive behaviors. But as the years went by, some of them crept back into my life and I had to deal with them once again because I had not dealt with some heart issues and had not renewed my way of thinking. I believe the worst addiction affecting the church right now is pornography. In a Barna study in 2016 in the US, one in three practicing, church-going Christians was seeking out porn on a regular basis. Even one in seven pastors and one in five youth pastors were using porn regularly. That doesn't mean this is just an issue guys deal with.

The number of women who use porn has been on the rise for years. Among females in the general population, 28 percent seek out porn regularly. Let those figures sink in. If you are included in this number, this book is for you.

By sharing my own story along the way, I want to show the process by which we become addicted, the various stages involved, and how the progression of addiction works. Then I want to demonstrate—in a unique way the Lord has shown me—how we can walk back out of addiction, or rather, how we can walk addiction out of us. I don't claim to have the magic bullet to defeat all addiction, but what I do have is a clear roadmap of the way in and the way out of addiction. It worked for me and I know it can work for you.

The first half of this book is about how we become addicted. The second is about how we heal and are restored. It may also be useful to those who are living with, or are close to, an addicted person. However, it will be most helpful if you are the person who has lost control of some aspect of your life. It was your journey that got you here. It can only be your journey that gets you out of here.

I do not refer to "addicts" in this little book; I never will. I believe we are people with a destiny that is much bigger than anything we're addicted to. It is an affront to our Creator to reduce the definition of a person to a single, diminishing word like addict. We are made by a loving God who always wanted us to be the men and women He had in his heart when He created us. But there is an enemy of our souls who wants to spoil God's plan for our lives. I want to look at how our very real enemy has used addiction against us to stall that plan. The enemy saw the greatness that God put in you and has tried everything to crush your confidence, to take away your voice, and to stop you discovering your true identity. You may feel broken and defeated, but take courage. The battle for your soul is not over, my friend. You can become the man who God created you to be.

I hope it will be enlightening for you as we go on a journey together to understand what happened to humanity from a spiritual perspective—how our lives got derailed, and how we can rediscover the wonderful life God had planned for us. It's not too late to recover the dreams you had before repeated failure gradually took them away. Perhaps they are not dead—just sleeping. This is an opportunity to awaken your dreams. We can still live the lives we always wanted to live.

1

THE CASTLE

I want you to imagine a castle—an old-fashioned castle with big stone walls, battlements, a moat, and a drawbridge. Fields surround it on every side. Inside the castle walls are smaller buildings and people going about their business. Up high, soldiers stand watch on the battlements. At the center is another fortified building known as a "keep." This is a well-defended tower with its own high walls and heavy doors. It is the center of power where the king of the castle lives.

Now I want you to imagine this castle is you. You are the castle. The outer walls are like your body. This is where you meet with the world outside. You need physical defenses to stop disease and injury from breaching your walls. You interface with the world through the five senses: sight, hearing, touch, smell, and taste. These are the gates of your castle.

Inside your castle walls is the realm of the soul. This cannot be seen from the outside. The soul is comprised of your mind, which controls your thinking and your imagination; your will, by which you make decisions; and your emotions, which create your feelings.

At the center of the castle is the keep. This is a castle within the castle. It has its own strong defenses. This is your heart. Not the muscle inside your chest, but the seat of your affections. The heart is defined by what we give our affections to, what we love, what we give our lives to. It is where, when things are working as they were intended, we hold the capacity to know right from wrong. It is where the conscience lies.

At the center of the keep, deep inside, is the throne room. It is the seat of power in our lives. The throne room is the source of truth, love, joy, and peace. This is where our spirit sits. Where we connect with God. Where we find our true identity. This is where the King sits.

A Christian is someone whose spirit is inhabited with God's spirit, and this can only happen when we are born again. We become a new creation with a new identity— we are "in Christ." So, we have God living at our center. He is the King of our castle. He is where the power, peace, love, and joy come from. His spirit joined to our spirit.

So far so good. I hope you can see this might be a useful way of looking at ourselves. On the outside is the body with its gates of the five senses, then the soul surrounding the heart, and finally, the spirit at the center.

I'm not the first person to use the analogy of a castle to explain our lives. *The Interior Castle*, or *The Mansions*, was written in 1577 by Teresa of Ávila, a Spanish Carmelite nun, as a guide for spiritual development. In it, she describes: "...a most beautiful crystal globe, made in the shape of a castle, and containing seven mansions, in the seventh and innermost of which was the King of Glory, in the greatest splendour, illumining and beautifying them all. The nearer one got to the centre, the stronger was the light; outside the palace limits everything was foul, dark and infested with toads, vipers and other venomous creatures." In his book *The Holy War* written in 1682, John Bunyan also used the analogy of a walled city to represent our soul's battle.

This book is a journey from the outside in to the center and back again. But it may not be what you expect. It's the journey taken by things that should not be there. Things that have invaded the castle and have taken over parts of it, sometimes as far as the keep—your heart, where they begin to take over your affections. Ultimately, these "things" want to reign from the throne room.

So, the question is: Is there anything in your castle that shouldn't be there?

2

———

UNDER ATTACK

From the moment mankind was on the planet, we have been under attack. God has great and good plans for us, but there is an enemy who is trying to ruin those plans. One thing you need to know is that your life has been under attack since you took your first breath—perhaps even before, when you were still in your mother's womb. We aren't really taught much about spiritual attack these days. Even in the church, we have tried to diagnose so many of our afflictions as having psychological or physical roots that we have stripped out any spiritual understanding behind our problems.

Jesus is really clear about the reality of an enemy attacking us. He calls him *the father of lies, the Devil, the thief, a murderer* who wants to *steal, kill and destroy.* He is the enemy of our souls.

I had a feeling when I was a little boy that I was in some way different. Unlike a lot of other kids, I had a grit that would not allow me to give up. In sports, I had no idea how to stop trying. I didn't understand why you would give up. It wasn't even about winning; it was about how you walked off the pitch, with your head held high or low. If I decided to do something, I would put absolutely everything into it. I didn't know then that I was to become a leader and that I would lead people through difficult times and places.

Even as a young boy, the enemy seemed to recognize this before I did myself. I was attacked verbally, I was attacked psychologically, and I was attacked physically. I had two older brothers. With one of them, I would regularly get into serious physical fights. There was always verbal abuse between us, and it was a constantly threatening environment. There were also fights and intimidation at school and in the town. I was physically attacked by bullies at school, and older men in town on several occasions. By my teenage years, I was able to defend myself, but it was miraculous that I survived without serious injury.

Looking back, I could see this was a tactic of the enemy to break my confidence and disrupt the calling on my life. I think of people in the Bible who had older brothers. Joseph was an arrogant young man and his brothers hated him. They hated him so much they were plotting to kill him. Instead, they sold him! David was good-looking and had been chosen over his older brothers by the prophet Samuel. His brothers ridiculed him publicly before he went out to fight Goliath. Sometimes the worst attacks come from our own families. The deepest wounds can be inflicted by those who are closest to us.

When we are young, attacks also come through authority figures—usually parents or teachers. Being told you will never amount to anything can carry such weight that it can set the course of a young life. Harsh words go deep, especially when you have not had time to develop defenses against them.

For me, I learned that if I stood up to bullies, they usually backed down. I responded to attacks by coming out fighting. Having failed to quash my determination with cruel words, violence and intimidation, the enemy changed course and tried a different tactic.

Question

Can you recognize a time in your early life where you were under attack from the enemy?

3

THE BREACH

THE ENEMY OF OUR SOULS, or the Devil, is interestingly also known as the "prince of the air," the "ruler of this world," and, as John says: *"...the whole world lies under the influence and misery of the Evil One"* (1 Jn 5:19 TPT). The implication here is that Satan is actually the one running the world. In the desert, he shows Jesus all the kingdoms of the world and tells Him: *"I will give you all authority and splendour for it has been given to me and I can give it to anyone I want to"* (Luke 4:6).

Another name for the Devil in Greek is *Diaballo*. This is a compound of two words: *dia*, which means "through," and *ballo*, meaning "I throw." This is where we get the word *diabolical*. The picture here is of one who relentlessly throws something until it breaks through.

Now I want you to consider your castle again. You have an enemy who has set up a siege against your castle. How does a siege work? The enemy surrounds the castle and starts a constant bombardment, hurling projectiles at the walls. As a young man, my physical body came under siege.

It is the body, its five senses—sight, hearing, smell, touch and taste—that begin to be assaulted with things from the outside world. In his book *The Holy War*, John Bunyan writes about the human soul as a city, Mansoul, which is under attack from the Devil. He tells us the city, our soul, has five gates called Eye-gate, Ear-gate, Nose-gate, Mouth-gate and Skin-gate. He also explains that the gates can only be breached if the occupants of the city open them *from the inside*. The enemy uses trickery, lies, and false promises to get us to open the doors of the castle. Here begins the long and relentless story of the temptation of the human soul. For some, however, I believe the doors can be forced open by others, especially when we are young. If you were physically, verbally, or sexually abused, this is a clear violation of your "castle."

I was given my first cigarette at 10 and my first alcoholic drink at the same age. Both my grandfathers came from Welsh mining villages. Coming from this culture, at 14 you left school and joined the men at work. The men in my family were not just allowed, but expected, to drink beer at home from the age of 14. By that age I had already drunk lots of beer. I had also tried marijuana. By 15 I was thrown out of school for making alcohol at home and selling it at school. I thought I was being an entrepreneur. They clearly didn't see it that way!

My young ears heard adults say things I assumed were true. I had no way of challenging what I heard as I had no alternative experience. Looking back, I was given terrible advice at various times in my life by older people. They basically invited me to taste, smell, and touch many things that I should never have been exposed to. My first experience with pornography was at the age of 14. I remember those images to this day. I had my first sexual encounter at 11 and my first girlfriend at 14.

When I initially tried something that was risky or I knew was wrong, my plan was to do it only once. My entire focus was on that first time. But once I had done it, well, I might as well do it again. And so, the thing I was only going to try once became normal. I liked the buzz, the physical sensation. I liked the thrill, the illicit part of it, the rebellious part of it. I liked the excitement of not getting caught, the ritual, the approval of the people I was doing it with. Encouraged by older people, while still a child, I began to do the things adults were doing around me.

Some of these things, like drinking, because it was approved of by older people, I had no problem with. But other things I flat-out knew were wrong. However, the exploration, fun, and sense of adventure overruled my conscience.

There is a chilling line in the book of Genesis where God is talking to a young man, Cain, just before he kills his brother. God gives him a choice:

…If you do what is right, will you not be accepted? But if you do not do what is right, sin is crouching at your door; it desires to have you, but you must rule over it (Genesis 4:7).

As a young man, sin was crouching at the door of my castle. It desired to have me. It had approached the gates of my castle, tempting my five senses, and I had let it in. What is interesting in the Genesis passage is that sin is not portrayed as something we do or "fall into." It is active, with a personality and a mission. It is strategic. It has a plan to breach our walls. It comes from the prince of the air, the ruler of this world, the world outside your castle where, as Teresa of Avila would say, "...everything was foul, dark and infested with toads, vipers and other venomous creatures."

Question

Can you recognize a time in your life when things got into your castle that shouldn't have been there?

4

THE FOOTHOLD

THE ENEMY USES THE ASSAULT on our gates (our senses) for one reason only: to get inside our castles. Once inside, what he really wants is to get at our emotions, to get at our thinking, and to get us to make wrong decisions. He is after our souls ultimately—our mind, will, and emotions.

The first thing he targets is our emotions. The amount of stimulus our bodies get once we give in to the first temptation deeply affects our emotions. We may feel guilty, but the pleasure and peer pressure outweigh the guilt and we go for it again.

The Emotions

Our society is obsessed with emotions. Entertainment is an obvious example of this. Sports, reality TV shows, even advertising, are full of emotive content.

I ran a design and marketing company for 23 years. There are entire industries out there spending billions of dollars trying to get us to respond emotionally to a product or service. There is such a thing as "emotional marketing." The main technique here, depending on the product, industry, and audience, is to define precisely what feeling you're aiming to elicit through marketing. This will influence the details of your marketing tactics, your copywriting, your media, your graphics, etc., to make it as effective as possible.

Studies show we rely far more on our feelings than on information when buying a product. Using emotional marketing encourages people to decide with their hearts, moreso than with their heads. Every TV channel is fighting for you attention. Everything we see as we swipe our phones is designed to create an emotional reaction. Not all of this is bad content, of course. But some is.

If we think of our castle again, the prince of the air is using our emotions to get us to make certain decisions all the time. We might call him the "prince of the airways" as he constantly bombards our castles with temptation. The world's relentless assault on our emotions can so impact us that it weakens our resolve and we subconsciously allow our feelings to lead us.

One of the foundational lies I believed is that my feelings were the same thing as the truth. As a result, my emotions ran my life. I would do what I FELT like doing. It led to a lack of discipline because my emotions would overrule my will. Even if I knew something was wrong, if I felt like doing it, I would go ahead. This led to a chaotic lifestyle.

As a young man, I would be driven by feelings to take drugs, chase women, take risks, be generally rebellious. What I only realized much later was that my emotions made very poor advisors. Basing decisions on what I was feeling frequently got me into trouble, and dangerous situations.

Question

In what ways have your emotions been targeted by the enemy?

The Will

In a mature person, the will is the gatekeeper in the castle, like a trained sentry guarding the gates, ready to make good decisions about what is let into the castle. However, the enemy's game plan here is to use our emotions to get us to make bad decisions, weakening our will in the process. This is a cunning technique because it bypasses our higher faculties. You can be an intelligent person who still makes bad decisions because you're making them based not on your thinking and your will, but on your feelings.

The human will is immensely powerful—so powerful that even God will not override it! He gave us free will. We are supposed to use our will to bring his will to the earth. Jesus taught us to pray, *"Your kingdom come, your will be done, on earth as it is in heaven."* But all too often we misuse our will and allow it to be hijacked, usually by making poor decisions based on our feelings. We allow the enemy to get in, and we don't use our will to defend our castle. Our will, lacking proper exercise, ceases to function as a gatekeeper. It sits emaciated while our underqualified, overfed emotions take over the job and open the gates.

Maybe you were brought up in a Christian home. Then you went to college. There you experienced "freedom" for the first time. No one to tell you what to do. The enemy spots you. The attack begins. There are parties. You want to fit in. You try alcohol, maybe even drugs. You get a boyfriend or girlfriend, and one thing leads to another. "Everyone is doing it." So, you do too.

It is by our will's repeated submission to outside influences that bad habits start to form in us. The enemy has breached our walls. And now he is on the inside, and *we* let him in. Sin was crouching at our door. We have not mastered it. We have let it in to the castle grounds. It has a foothold.

My will had been compromised so often that it had become weak—barely operational. I would wake up with regrets from the night before and be determined not to do the same things again. By the end of the same day, I was back in the bar with my friends, smoking, drinking, taking drugs and partying. During my twenties, this went on for years. There is a phrase: "The road to hell is paved with good intentions." I had plenty of good intentions but lacked the strength of will to carry them out.

My will had been misused because it was taking directions from my emotions and from my darkened thinking, not from my spirit. I was looking to the world for guidance and so would be swayed into going along with what everyone else was doing, or by whatever I felt like doing. I lacked the inner strength to determine my own action. The gates to my castle were wide open. My gatekeeper was drunk at his post.

Question

Can you think of a time when you have made bad decisions based on your emotions?

5

THE STRONGHOLD

NOW THE ATTACK ON THE mind starts. By this point, it doesn't even feel like an attack. It's just a matter of agreeing with what other people are saying. It's just adopting a worldly view. After all, it's a logical way of thinking. Everyone believes this way. Surely they're "enlightened." The influence of western philosophy and the devaluing of the biblical narrative in modern society have all taken their toll.

This is nothing new. The rejection of the wisdom of God contains a spiritual aspect, and it was the same in biblical times. In his letter to the the church in Ephesus, St. Paul explains the consequences of the mindset in the culture at the time—how it had become darkened because of the hardening of their hearts:

So I tell you this, and insist on it in the Lord, that you must no longer live as the Gentiles do, in the futility of their thinking. They are darkened in their understanding and separated from the life of God because of the ignorance that is in them due to the hardening of their hearts. Having lost all sensitivity, they have given themselves over to sensuality so as to indulge in every kind of impurity, and they are full of greed (Ephesians 4:17-19).

In this way, as our minds become veiled to the truth of God's word, we begin to construct ways of thinking that justify our behavior and decisions.

Now we are entering a new level of danger. We have allowed our understanding to be darkened. This is where denial starts to manifest in our thinking. We think of ways to actually defend what the enemy is doing in our castles. We use intellectualism, humor, denial, distractions, even anger to keep away anyone who challenges our behavior. We withdraw from those who love us, who are close enough to confront us. We want our "freedom."

We think of ways to actually defend what the enemy is doing in our castles. The round turrets on the corners of a castle are not just a nice design feature; they allow the watchmen on the walls to see along the length of the straight walls below them. They are designed to eliminate any blind spots where the enemy can hide. Denial creates blind spots along your castle walls.

A stronghold is built when you create a narrative of thought, words and behavior to defend enemy activity in your castle. These strongholds always have a lie at their foundation.

One of my strongholds was built upon the lie that I was independent and free to do what I wanted. I would defend my freedom at all costs. My will was totally bent to protecting it. I was self-righteous and stubborn about it. My mind argued that my freedom was paramount. But the truth was that freedom without discipline is toxic and actually leads to bondage. My feelings had become overfed and dominant. My will was being misused. Instead of keeping the gates closed, my emotions were telling my will to open the gates and let in whatever made me feel good, because it was my right.

I got to the point in my life where the faculties of my soul—my mind, will and emotions—were all now conspiring to reinforce my faulty thinking and behavior, and to defend it. Now, instead of defending against the enemy, I was defending the enemy himself. My soul was now actually protecting the infiltrator that had wormed its way inside. I had begun to build a stronghold.

The stronghold becomes a tower within the castle grounds that is established in direct opposition to the keep, wherein lies truth and power. We develop *"arguments and every pretension that sets itself up against the knowledge of God"* (2 Corinthians 10:5). Each lie we have believed becomes the foundation of a tower in the grounds of the castle that should not be there. These stronghold towers create blind spots and shadows in the castle. They are made to conceal lies. The enemy hides there, operating out of and defending the strongholds. They were built so you could live in shadow instead of light. If anyone approaches a stronghold in someone's life, they will usually be aggressively rebuffed. If you challenge a foundational lie in someone's life, you will find out just how hard the enemy will fight to defend the stronghold.

Have you ever noticed how defensive someone with an addiction is? If you call them on it, they will flare up, or just leave, and you won't see them for months afterward. You end up "walking on eggshells" around them. Have you ever noticed how emotionally manipulative someone with an addiction is? They will become extremely emotional, they may self-harm, or even threaten suicide. Have you ever noticed how a person with an addiction can lie to your face about their secret activities? Have you ever noticed how they can run rings around you with words and arguments? Have you ever noticed how bad their decisions are?

The strongholds that can develop in our castles become bridgeheads from which the enemy launches the next attack—and the next attack is on the keep itself. Sin wants to enter our hearts. It wants a seat at the table of our affections.

Questions

Can you think of examples in which you have constructed ways of thinking to justify your bad behavior and decisions?

Can you think of any foundational lies you've believed about yourself or about God?

6

HEART ATTACK

NOW THAT THE ENEMY HAS us forming habits and building strongholds, he'll go after the keep. He is going after our hearts. He wants us to create a space in our hearts for the things we're becoming addicted to, the things we cannot and will not give up, because now we love them. He wants to establish sin in our hearts. The sin that was once crouching at our door desiring to have us now has us.

As well as being the seat of our affections, the heart is also where our conscience lives, where we know deep down what is right and wrong. And it's also the place the Spirit of God is closest to. So herein lies the dilemma: How do you live with your conscience, and with God, when your heart is compromised?

I remember getting to the point where the things I had let into my heart were so important that I would sacrifice relationships for them. By the time I was 18 I had left home and was living on my own in Paris. I had a 24-year-old American girlfriend and I was mixing with people much older than me. I was working for a man who I found out later was a drug dealer. There was high quality cocaine everywhere. I soon got hooked. It was the most seductive drug I had ever taken. It made me feel like a king. I became devious and prioritized my supply. It quickly came to have a special place in my heart. I loved it more than even the people closest to me. Instead of guarding my heart, I was guarding the "white lady."

However, part of me also hated it at the same time. That's because even though I had allowed it in and given it a seat at the table of my affections, it was never supposed to be there. Deep down, even though I had come to love the thing I was now addicted to, I didn't love what was happening to me, and my conscience was still telling me it was wrong. This created inner turmoil. I felt guilty; I was doing things I knew were wrong. My conscience was still working, it was still trying to fight the enemy that was now inside the keep of my castle.

The Conscience

I believe our conscience—our facility to tell right from wrong—is hard wired. Human beings are made in the image of a God of justice who cares deeply about doing the right thing. I never had to tell my children what "it's not fair" means. They would tell me. If one child had two of something and the other had only one, I would hear the words *"it's not fair."* The basic knowledge of justice seems to be built into us. This natural capacity for telling right from wrong can be filled with either good moral teaching and examples or with bad ones, but we have that capacity in us.

Working well, the conscience is like a knife, able to accurately separate good from bad. But if we go against it enough times, it simply becomes blunt. Our conscience becomes less useful to us as a moral guide; it gets compromised. If it comes up against the power of a mind in denial, of consistent lies and duplicity, it will become "seared" as St. Paul describes it. At a young age I compromised my conscience in many ways, but one incident did enormous damage to me and to others.

At the age of 19 I got my girlfriend pregnant. She told me she wanted an abortion. I knew this was wrong. I wasn't a Christian, but I knew deep in my heart this wasn't right. But because I loved her and was afraid of losing the relationship, I didn't challenge her. Instead, I paid a French doctor and I held her hand when it was done.

It felt like I had finally crossed the line. I had taken a human life. It broke my heart. How could I ever recover from this? The guilt was awful and I anesthetized myself further with drugs and drink. The relationship broke up anyway when I was 21, and I went into a huge depression. I fell apart. I got panic attacks and agoraphobia. I was so afraid that I couldn't leave the house for about three months. I remember sitting on my bed thinking, This is when I get the gun out (and I had a 12-gauge in the cupboard). As I thought that, a voice inside me said, NO WAY! It was so strong that I obeyed and gave up the idea of ending my life. I hung on and gradually got better but was numb and mildly depressed for years afterward.

I got back into work and kept my mind busy. I became good at what I did and ended up in London with a great job. I partied to kill the emotional pain and guilt that was the background hum to my life. The irony was, I had all the world had to offer. I was working as production controller of Vogue Magazine by the time I was 25, handling a budget of five million. I owned a flat in London, had money and all the trappings of a hedonistic lifestyle. But as Thomas Merton once said, "People may spend their whole lives climbing the ladder of success only to find, once they reach the top, that the ladder is leaning against the wrong wall." Jesus put in another way. He said: *"For what use is it to gain all the wealth and power of this world, with everything it could offer you, at the cost of your own life?"* (Mark 8:36 TPT).

Inside, I was like a man starving in a desert. My spirit was dying. By the time I was 27 my liver was not processing alcohol anymore—I was sick. I would go to work, then come home and smoke hashish on my own just to dull the pain.

Question

Can you think of a time when you may have compromised your conscience?

The only way I could live with the damage I had done was to harden my heart. I no longer wanted to hear my conscience; I had to stifle it. It was the only survival technique I had. The trouble is that once we harden our hearts and no longer pay attention to our conscience, it becomes blunt and stops working altogether.

Jesus said in Matthew 13:15: *For this people's heart has become calloused; they hardly hear with their ears, and they have closed their eyes. Otherwise, they might see with their eyes, hear with their ears, understand with their hearts and turn, and I would heal them.*

Remember the words from Paul's letter to the Ephesians: *They are darkened in their understanding and separated from the life of God because of the ignorance that is in them due to the hardening of their hearts* (Ephesians 4:18).

Even as Christians we can harden our heart to our conscience and to God. We turn away inwardly from his influence, from his Word, from his people. If we ever prayed, it gets harder and more desperate. If we were going to church, it gets more awkward and we must put up a front every Sunday. Outwardly we are "fine" as we tell anyone who asks. Inwardly we are deeply conflicted.

Question

Do you think your heart has become hardened?
In what ways?

Compartmentalization

The only way we can live and function in this way with such inner conflict is to compartmentalize our lives. It shook me recently, finding out about another high-profile Christian leader who had been involved in sexual immorality. I was shaken but I was not surprised. I wasn't judging them. But I had two questions. The first was, how could someone so intelligent live in such denial? I began to realize intelligence is no defense against sin. In fact, it may even help in building strongholds—the intellectual defenses we construct to justify immoral behavior. The second question was, at what point did they lose their fear of God? Moses told the Israelites during the exodus that *"...the fear of God will be with you to keep you from sinning."* When we behave in such ways and we don't let the fear of God stop us, we are truly in trouble.

The fact is that this is not a "slippery slope." It is a very gradual, almost imperceptible descent that may take years to walk down until we find we have left the narrow path that leads to life and we are walking on the wide path that leads to destruction (Matthew 7:13-14).

One of my prayers recently is, "God, increase my fear of you—I never want to lose it, Lord."

Our ability to build strongholds and compartmentalize our lives is extraordinary. But these lead to hypocrisy and living a miserable double life.

Question

Do you think your heart has become compartmentalized? In what areas?

If we are chronically addicted, the soul is now conspiring with the enemy to defend the bad things that have been given a place in our hearts. All the soul, mind, will and emotions are defending our behavior. The castle is overrun.

For most people who struggle with just one area of their life, we compartmentalize it. Outwardly we seem to be functioning well. Inwardly we are conflicted, with a divided heart, double-minded and miserable. I was like this at times—high functioning but addicted, holding down good jobs, but leading a double life.

7

IDENTITY THEFT

WHAT I DIDN'T REALIZE was that the real attack was not on my body, or my soul. It wasn't even on my heart. The real attack was on my identity. The enemy was terrified of me finding out who I really was.

Identity theft has become big business in the criminal world. Like most crimes, it's not an original idea. It was first perpetrated in the Garden of Eden. The original thief is Satan. Jesus tells us that he comes to steal, kill, and destroy (John 10:10).

The endgame in these attacks on your body, soul, and heart is to get to the throne room of the castle and to steal your true identity as a child of God and make us believe that we are orphans.

The enemy was terrified of me finding out who I really was.

The good news is that the enemy can't change our identity if we are in Christ. We are told that as Christians, we are sealed with the Holy Spirit (Ephesians 1:13). God's own

Spirit comes to indwell, or take up residence, in the believer. The Holy Spirit identifies God's people as his inheritance. The Holy Spirit provides the inward assurance that we belong to God as his children. God has adopted us (Rom 8:15). Because we are God's sons and daughters, He sent his Spirit "into our hearts," the Spirit who calls out "Abba, Father" (Galatians 4:6).

So, the attack is not directly on our spirit, which is sealed with God's spirit; it is on our spirituality. It is on our understanding of who we are. When Jesus was in the desert, the Devil began two of the temptations with the words, *"If you are the Son of God…"* He was directly trying to sow doubt in Jesus's mind about who He really was. He wanted Jesus to doubt the fact that God was his father.

The Orphan Spirit

Right from the beginning, God has wanted to make us his children. The Devil has wanted to make us orphans.

In Genesis chapter 3 we are told: *Now the serpent was more crafty than any of the wild animals the LORD God had made. He said to the woman, "Did God really say, 'You must not eat from any tree in the garden'?" The woman said to the serpent, "We may eat fruit from the trees in the garden, but God did say, 'You must not eat fruit from the tree that is in the middle of the garden, and you must not touch it, or you will die.'" "You will not certainly die," the serpent said to the woman. "For God knows that when you eat from it your eyes will be opened, and you will be like God, knowing good and evil."*

When Satan tempted them, he was tempting them to rebel against God. This changes the parent-child relationship. It makes them "equal to God" and not needing his covering, his guidance, and his authority over them.

In his rebellion, Satan had already decided he would have no one over him. He set himself up against God and wanted to rule. He wanted his own kingdom, with no one in authority over him. He did not want a Father. He is the original rebellious spirit. He is the original orphan spirit. In tempting Adam and Eve, he wanted them to become like him. When Adam and Eve were pushed out of the Garden of Eden, they became spiritual orphans. And because mankind was separated from God, we all became orphans.

The world is now a giant orphanage *"...in which you used to live when you followed the ways of this world and of the ruler of the kingdom of the air, the spirit who is now at work in those who are disobedient..."* (Ephesians 2:2). It is dominated by orphan thinking and behavior. Rife with disobedience, independence, individualism, rebellion, oppression of the poor, loneliness, anxiety, fear, lust, guilt, shame, division, jealousy, disease, and ultimately death. We see this in both individuals and in organizations.

What the enemy wants is for you to redefine yourself in his terms. That's why the scripture, *"For as he thinks in his heart, so is he…"* (Proverbs 23:7), is so powerful. The way you live your life will depend on who you think you are.

The enemy wants to create orphan thinking. He wants

us to think we have no Father in heaven. He wants us to think we're alone, that we need to fight other people to get our share on earth. He wants us to be self-reliant, defensive, aggressive, and obsessed with earthly things. He wants us to build and reinforce our identity as an orphan.

Question

Do you recognize this orphan spirit in yourself?

The Good News is that God wants you to know you are not an orphan. That He will not leave us as orphans, but He will come to us. Jesus came to deal with the Devil and destroy the works of the enemy (John 3:8).

My life was full of broken relationships, broken promises and broken dreams. I was living a life ruled by the orphan spirit and I had come to a desperate place in my life. I was so disillusioned with the world, so disappointed with myself and other people, that at the age of 27, I went on a search—for the truth. I was determined to find something good, something true, something I could trust. I began to read, and my reading eventually took me to the Bible. I also had a friend who was praying for me. In fact, I found out later she had her whole home group praying for me. One weekend she took me to a Christian retreat center. It was there that my life changed.

It was on a beautiful May morning that I put my hand on the door of a small chapel in Oxfordshire and said, "God, I know you are good and I want you in my life." Then something extraordinary happened. As I went in, there were six young people in the chapel singing in tongues. But I heard at least twelve voices. It was as if the heavens had opened and I could hear singing from heaven. I fell to my knees and wept as God poured his love into my heart. I had never experienced anything like it. I had not cried for ages. My heart had become so hard over those reckless years.

On that day in May, I was reborn. God filled me with his Spirit. He gave me hope, filled me with love, joy, peace, purpose and meaning. And He took the guilt away. The very next day, back in London, I walked around the park and it was as if Jesus was walking beside me. I could feel his presence. I told Him everything that happened, and the guilt that had been weighing me down left me. I realized then that He had taken it. I finally understood that He came to pay the price on the cross for the things I could never pay for. He took my guilt and shame.

I gave it all up—moved out of London, started training as a youth worker. Within two years I was on staff at a church. Then I started working in prisons. In the world's eyes, I had gone from the heights to the depths, but God was there as I went to the depths of society—the Holy Spirit, like water, naturally flows to the lowest places. As I followed Him onto the streets and into the prisons, I saw hundreds turn to Him and saw their lives totally change. He has taken me all over the world since that day. I have been in dozens of prisons from Norway to Nigeria, from Poland to Panama. Some of them are hell holes, but I have seen God at work in all of them and learned that no one is beyond his reach.

I wasn't beyond his reach and neither are you. He loves you. Jesus came not to judge the world but to save it. He reached me when I had come to the end of myself and was in the depths of a chaotic, selfish lifestyle. You might feel like you're dying inside today, but know this: Christianity was born in a tomb. Jesus went in dead and came out alive. Only God can bring us back to life.

If you don't know Him, cry out to Him. He will hear you and He will answer you with love. He is just a prayer away… Today is the day when you can know the wonderful God who already knows you and loves you.

8

CRISIS

MY ADDICTIVE BEHAVIOR STOPPED WHEN I gave my life to God at the age of 27. But after a few years, old habits began to creep back in. Even though my spirit had been born again, my mind, will, and emotions had not been renewed in the same way. After the initial "honeymoon period" with God, the attacks intensified. The enemy activity increased to try to stop me from entering my destiny and calling from God.

It's hard to say when this happened because it was so gradual. I was married with two kids. My more obvious addictions had been dealt with—I hadn't taken drugs or had a drink or a cigarette for over 10 years. But I was using sexual fantasy as an escape from the reality of life. As a result, I was constantly tempted to look at pornography. I would regularly flirt with it on TV and social media. It had become a continual problem.

This was a very difficult situation. I was now deeply conflicted—even more than I had been before I knew

God. Being addicted when you're out there in the world is one thing. Being addicted as a Christian is another. The guilt was worse. The remorse was continual. The sense that I was letting God and others down was awful. It's so contrary to the life I knew I should have been living that the only option was to hide it—to compartmentalize it and to construct a stronghold of lies around it that justified my behavior.

A few years ago I was traveling regularly to Poland, working in the prisons. My Polish friends came to visit me in the UK and brought with them as a gift a large coffee table book about Poland. In it, there is a chapter on Polish castles. Leafing through the book, I found myself becoming deeply moved as I saw one castle after another in ruins. Over the centuries, they had been attacked and left to deteriorate and decay. You could only imagine their former glory. I realized I had let my castle be gradually taken over and it too had begun its descent to ruin.

If we are being truthful, many Christians find themselves in this situation. We have allowed ourselves to be compromised in one way or another. I believe it is a largely unspoken crisis in the church.

At this point I want to encourage us. We so typically think of sin as something we do, often repeatedly. We think we are just "sinful" and can't stop sinning. I had failed so many times—repented so many times, confessed to friends, so many times… However, the Bible talks of sin as having a personality and a plan. It *"desires to have you"* (Genesis

4:6), it *"seizes the opportunity,"* it *"deceives,"* it has *"slaves,"* it *"lives in us,"* and it wants to *"reign"* in us (see Romans 6 and 7). So, I want to offer the idea that something like an addictive habit is not just something we do but rather, a particular strategy of the enemy. The enemy saw greatness in you, before you did. He was terrified of you realizing your potential and so assaulted your castle. Yes, we have somehow colluded with it and let it in, but what follows is how we can take responsibility and begin to master it. We can rule over it. We do not have to live like this anymore.

Despite my situation, I knew enough about God to know there must be a way out. I had tasted freedom and I knew there must be more. I started to cry out for real wisdom, for the way out. At this point, several events happened that revealed the nature of the battle I was in. God stepped in and began to speak to me through scripture, dreams and prophetic words to reveal the truth of my condition. What follows is an illustration of how God wants to help us once we turn to Him in desperation.

I fell asleep listening to the Bible on an app one night. In a dream I was sitting with a pastor friend of mine and he was speaking the words from Jeremiah 30:12-15, which I was actually hearing from the app.

"For thus says the LORD:
'Your affliction is incurable,
Your wound is severe.
There is no one to plead your cause,
That you may be bound up;

You have no healing medicines.
All your lovers have forgotten you;
They do not seek you;
For I have wounded you with the wound of an enemy,
With the chastisement of a cruel one,
For the multitude of your iniquities,
Because your sins have increased.
Why do you cry about your affliction?
Your sorrow is incurable.
Because of the multitude of your iniquities,
Because your sins have increased,
I have done these things to you.

I woke utterly shocked. This shook me to the core. I had an incurable wound. There was no medicine for me. "All my lovers had forgotten me…". The fantasy life I had been living was just that—a fantasy. I grabbed my Bible and read on…

'Therefore, all those who devour you shall be devoured;
And all your adversaries, every one of them, shall go into captivity;
Those who plunder you shall become plunder,
And all who prey upon you I will make a prey.
For I will restore health to you
And heal you of your wounds,' says the LORD…"
(Jeremiah 30:16-17).

Even though my wound was serious and "incurable" by myself or by the world, God was going to restore my health. He was going to bring my enemies into captivity. The thief who had been robbing me will be robbed, the enemy that has been stalking me will be stalked. God will heal my wounds Himself. I learned then that God was leading this process of healing me.

I started to dream a lot in this time when God had revealed my "incurable wound" and then promised to heal me. He was revealing blind spots.

I dreamt I saw a woman sitting on the edge of a field on a blanket on her own. I climbed over the fence and went over to talk to her. I was using all my charm to engage her in conversation.

She looked at me and said, "Did I give you any signals that I wanted you to talk to me?"

"No," I replied.

The dream then switched to me in a house with her. She was watching me pack my bag and leave. It was embarrassing. It was absolutely clear that not a single part of my attention was called for or welcomed.

...All your lovers have forgotten you;
They do not seek you; ...

I woke up. In the dream, I had seen with my eyes, decided to approach, used all my charm and cunning to engage this woman. What was in my heart?

Iniquity is sin or immoral behavior. But transgression is an act of violating a law, command or duty. I had transgressed. In my dream, I had literally "crossed the fence" (crossed the line) and was using my charm to engage in unwanted attention. Jesus is clear on this matter:

"Thou shalt not commit adultery: But I tell you that anyone who looks at a woman lustfully has already committed adultery with her in his heart" (Matthew 5: 27-28).

Just by thinking about these things, I was crossing the line. I was transgressing. The dream was exposing what was in my heart and what I was thinking. It was sobering, especially when I realized Jesus had paid a great price for our transgressions and our sin. My thinking about these things had cost him dearly. *But he was pierced for our transgressions, he was crushed for our iniquities; the punishment that brought us peace was on him, and by his wounds we are healed* (Isaiah 53:5).

Within a few days of this, an old friend of ours called my wife. We hadn't been in contact for years, but she and my wife started to pray together. She had a picture for our family:

"I see a large room, with sunlight streaming in. There is someone in the room dancing with a giant. It looks like an intimate scene, but the giant is looking down at the person with hatred in his eyes. The giant is holding both the person's hands with fingers interlaced. I have no idea what this means…"

When my wife told me this, I knew exactly what it meant. Our house is full of light; it is a good place. But I was dancing with a giant who hated me. Every time I indulged in sexual fantasy I was dancing with this giant. It looked like a romantic scene, but it was not. And it had me in its grip. If you link your two hands together now by interlinking your fingers, you will find that if you squeeze one hand hard and try to release the other, it is a very strong grip. It is a strong hold. It is a stronghold.

This giant had me in a stronghold. I had allowed it into my castle. I had allowed it in through my senses. It had won my emotions. I had conspired with it to create thinking that justified my behavior, leading me to make consistently bad decisions. It had invaded my castle. I had even given it a place in my heart. Now, it was after my identity.

I was broken hearted when I found out this is what had happened to me. I began to realize the enemy had been attacking me, had tempted me, used my emotions, twisted my thinking, and taken away my ability to make good decisions. I started to get angry at what I had let happen. I wanted my castle back. It was my castle.

This giant had me in a stronghold...It had invaded my castle. I had even given it a place in my heart. Now, it was after my identity.

God gave it to me to look after and to build a thriving community from. I had let Him down. I had let things in that should never be there.

Questions

Have you reached a crisis where you have had enough?

Do you want your identity back?

Do you want your castle back?

If you want your heart back, if you want your identity back, if you want your castle back—read on.

The Way Out

In the 1980s and early 1990s there was a campaign against drugs in the US, built around the simple three-word slogan, JUST SAY NO. This is a valid idea, as long as you aren't addicted to anything. You can resist if there is no breach in your walls. For someone who already has a pernicious habit, JUST SAY NO is useless. If the enemy is already in your castle, you have probably already begun to construct a way of thinking that makes it okay for you to JUST SAY YES!

This is where most Christian teaching on temptation begins and ends. The message is: "Just resist—just say no." There are lots of wonderful scriptures that are often quoted from the pulpit about temptation.

No temptation has overtaken you except what is common to mankind. And God is faithful; he will not let you be tempted beyond what you can bear. But when you are tempted, he will also provide a way out so that you can endure it (1 Corinthians 10:13).

I believe this scripture is true. The trouble is, these scriptures begin to lose their power in the lives of an addicted person because they have been so compromised by sin and failed so many times that the words have seemed to stop working. The word of God must be coupled with faith to be effective.

…but the word which they heard did not profit them, not being mixed with faith in those who heard it (Hebrews 4:2).

For someone who has failed repeatedly, it is their faith that starts to diminish, weakening the power of the word in their lives. This is not a failure of the word of God; it is a failure of our faith.

There is also a strategic problem here. This is because we're encouraged to resist and to defend our castles when we should be attacking. You need to defend when an enemy is attacking you from the outside. But when the enemy is on the inside, you need to mount an offense from within.

If an enemy has already breached the castle keep, it is no good closing the gates and putting watchmen on the walls to see if there is any trouble coming. We need to strike the enemy where he lies entrenched and drive him out, across the castle grounds and out through the gates. Once he has been driven out, then we can go into defense mode.

When Jesus was in the desert being tempted by the Devil, he was on the enemy's turf. He defended himself with scripture. However, when He went to Jerusalem, the Holy City, to the temple and saw that the corruption of the world had entered there, He did not quote scripture to defend his position. If the walled city of Jerusalem is like a castle, then the temple is the heart and the Holy of Holies in the temple is the throne room. Jesus saw that the moneychangers were in the heart of the city—inside the temple courts. They were now on his turf. So, what did He do? He went on the attack. He made a whip of cords and drove out the moneychangers, overturning their tables, crying, *"My house will be called a house of prayer, but you are making it a den of robbers"* (Matthew 21:13).

For this reason, breaking an addiction does not start with resisting; it starts with attacking. And it starts not from the castle walls but from the throne room. The way out is the way in—in reverse.

So, if we look at the structure of this book and see the progress of sin in our lives, so far it looks like this:

The castle

Under attack

The breach (body)

The foothold (soul)

The stronghold (mind)

Heart attack (heart)

Identity theft

So, to reverse the order would look like this:

Reestablish our identity

Reclaim our hearts

Renew our minds

Restore our souls

Strengthen our bodies

The castle defended

The castle restored

My proposition may seem counterintuitive because it is not to immediately defend ourselves from attacks. We don't start by standing on the walls and just saying no! This is ineffectual. We must begin in the throne room—in the center—to establish our true identity by establishing who is on the throne.

Once this has begun, we can move out and reclaim our hearts and slay any giants we have been dancing with in our castles. If we don't establish who is in control, we will be fighting from a weak and defeated position. Renewing our minds and restoring our souls come next, clearing out the rest of the castle by taking orders from the King, following our consciences, and using God's authority and wisdom to lead us to fill our hearts and minds with his love and his words and to make good decisions. We will be healing as we go. Then we can re-instate the defenses and defend our castle.

We must begin in the throne room—in the center—to establish our true identity by establishing who is on the throne.

The reason I think it is important to get our castles back in this order is because if we don't take back control of the throne room, we will be standing on the walls, looking for attacks, and yet continuing to leave the back door open at night. We will still be "dancing with the enemy" and we will not have established who is in control and whose orders we are following.

It is quite likely we will, for example, put internet blockers on our devices, but a few days later we will access the web for inappropriate content via an app that is not covered by the software. We are smart. We will find a way around our own defenses on the walls, while the enemy is still encamped inside the castle.

So, let's start in the throne room.

9

REESTABLISH YOUR IDENTITY

There are some things we need to know about ourselves. If we have blind spots concealing our shortcomings from us, they can also make us blind to the good things about ourselves. Part of the enemy's tactics is to get us to see ourselves as hopeless sinners (even if we have been saved by grace). God doesn't see us that way. He says we are the *"righteousness of God"* (2 Corinthians 5:21). He says we are already *"raised up and seated with Christ in heavenly places"* (Ephesians 2:6).

When God began to take me on this journey where I was having sobering dreams about my transgressions, I was also having amazing dreams about fulfilling my calling in God. These dreams reminded me of the calling on my life to bring the love of God to those around me and to lead people out of oppressive and dark situations. During this season, I began writing down all the scriptures that had been spoken prophetically over me. I would regularly revisit these and read them out to remind myself of the words God had spoken over me. I wanted to see his view of me. I wanted to live toward the reality of my destiny.

In Paul's first letter to Timothy, he tells him to use the prophecies that were spoken over his life *"as weapons as you wage spiritual warfare by faith and with a clean conscience"* (1 Timothy 1:18 TPT). By speaking these words out loud, I was declaring the truth to all the angels and demons and staking my ground. I used them as weapons and prayed over them. It was not enough just to read a word about me—I had to pray to make it come to pass. I was beginning to reestablish my identity.

Your Lineage

You will never know who you are until you know whose you are.

Our parents knew nothing about us before we were born. They may not have even known if we were a boy or a girl. But God conceived us in his mind before our parents conceived us in their bodies. God knew us before we were born. God is our real father.

"Before I formed you in the womb I knew you, before you were born I set you apart (Jeremiah 1:5). Psalm 139:13 tells us: *For you created my inmost being; you knit me together in my mother's womb.*

It was when the Father breathed his spirit into Adam that he came alive. The word for breath in Hebrew is Ruach—the same word as Spirit. We are alive because

God breathed life into us. *The Lord God formed the man from the dust of the ground and breathed into his nostrils the breath of life and the man became a living being* (Genesis 2:7).

We are primarily a spirit with a soul, in a body, not as the world would have you believe—a body with a mind and maybe, somewhere, a soul. I experienced this graphically a few years ago when I held my brother's hand as he breathed his last breath on earth. When you experience someone dying and see their body after they have passed away, you become fully aware that the body is not them. Something has left their body—their essence, their spirit—and it leaves a shell, which is the body. It's why we call them "the departed," not "the stopped." We don't say, "He stopped." We say, "He's gone."

Job says, *"as long as I have life within me, the breath of God in my nostrils"* (Job 27:3).

Adam and Eve, full of the spirit, walked with God in the cool of the day—communing with Him. This is what we were designed to do. We were meant to live in joy and deep ongoing relationship with the Father who created us, with nothing between us, spirit to Spirit, where we know only acceptance, peace, and love continually. This was God's plan for us.

But as we know, Adam and Eve sinned, and were expelled from the garden. They died spiritually and eventually physically. The deep spiritual connection with the Father was broken. This is the great tragedy of our lives. Even in each of our own stories, there came a time when we lost our innocence. We were thrown into this world where, if we were not protected adequately, the enemy was allowed to influence us into believing and behaving like orphans.

But Jesus came to *"destroy the works of the Devil"* (1 John 3:8). If the Devil's plan was to make us misidentify ourselves and to behave like orphans, then what Jesus said in John 14 makes perfect sense: *"I will not leave you as orphans; I will come to you"*. Jesus came to bring us back into the same relationship He had with the Father—to be one with God. He did it by breathing The Spirit of God back into us.

A Christian is someone who believes Jesus is the risen Son of God and who has asked God to come into their life. *"If you declare with your mouth, 'Jesus is Lord,' and believe in your heart that God raised him from the dead, you will be saved"* (Romans 10:9). The result of this is that we have God's spirit who comes to live inside us. Jesus describes this as being *"born again."* We become a new creation with a new identity—we are *"in Christ"* as God's Spirit is breathed back into us. We have God living at our center. He is where the power, peace, love, and joy come from. His Spirit joined to our spirit.

Don't you know that you yourselves are God's temple and that God's Spirit dwells in your midst? (1 Corinthians 3:16).

This is how we know that we live in him and he in us: He has given us of his Spirit (1 John 4:13).

Jesus came to restore our original relationship with God: We are no longer orphans. We are children of God, filled with his Spirit once again.

Prayer

Lord, I thank you that you conceived me and have loved me since the beginning of time. You sent your son Jesus to rescue me from sin and death. I am your precious child. I thank you that you have saved me. You have a plan for my life. I am fearfully and wonderfully made. I reject any identity that the enemy has put on me. From this day I commit to see myself and to speak of myself as a son (or daughter) of the Most High King. Establish my identity in you, Lord.

(Psalm 139, John 3:16, Jeremiah 29:11, Romans 8:14).

Your Responsibility

So far, I have stated that addiction is an example of the enemy's strategy to keep you from your destiny. However, this doesn't mean we do not have responsibility for ourselves. When God questioned Adam and Eve about their sin, Adam didn't take responsibility; he blamed Eve. Eve then blamed the serpent. In passing on the responsibility for their actions, they also passed on the authority over themselves.

"Have you eaten from the tree of which I commanded you not to eat?" And the man answered, "The woman whom You gave me, she gave me fruit from the tree, and I ate it." Then the LORD God said to the woman, "What is this you have done?" "The serpent deceived me," she replied, "and I ate." (Genesis 3: 11-13).

The serpent, crafty as he was, said nothing. He took the responsibility—and he took the authority. Legitimate authority is given. But authority can be taken (stolen). We see this where society and individuals use force and violence to rule over others. They set up counterfeit systems of authority. This is what Satan has done on earth.

The enemy wants us to have a victim mentality. In this state, we will blame everything and everyone else for our problems, including an addiction. When we are not taking full responsibility, we will never have authority over our castle.

Your Authority

Jesus has all authority on heaven and earth. He is over all other authority, powers, and dominion.

He raised Him from the dead and seated Him at His right hand in the heavenly realms, far above all rule and authority, power and dominion, and every name that is named, not only in the present age but also in the one to come. And God put everything under His feet and made Him head over everything for the church, which is His body, the fullness of Him who fills all in all (Ephesians 1:20-23).

"All authority in heaven and on earth has been given to me…" (Matt 28:18). Jesus delegates parts of his authority to his sons and daughters. Specifically, to deal with sickness and demons, and to deliver the gospel message.

Then Jesus called the Twelve together and gave them power and authority over all demons, and power to cure diseases. And He sent them out to proclaim the kingdom of God and to heal the sick (Luke 9:1).

At this point you might think He was just delegating his authority to the disciples. However, later, Jesus sends out 72 more of his followers:

After this, the Lord appointed seventy-two others and sent them two by two ahead of Him to every town and place He was about to visit… "Heal the sick who are there and tell them, 'The kingdom of God is near you.'…" (Luke 10: 1,9).

As his followers, we too have been delegated his authority. If you think about it, God sent Jesus to give us a spirit of adoption and to bring us home to the Father. We are not hired servants; we are his children. For much of my Christian life it has felt like I was on God's property, but I was skulking around the outbuildings trying to look busy and stay out of trouble. All the time God wanted me seated at the family table, planning the family business. I am his son, not a servant. In Luke 15, we see the prodigal son who was given a ring by the father. That was the signet ring. This carried the family seal. It gave the son authority to carry out the family business.

For much of my Christian life it has felt like I was on God's property, but I was skulking around the outbuildings trying to look busy and stay out of trouble. All the time God wanted me seated at the family table, planning the family business.

We are seated with Christ, in the spirit, in the throne room. But God has given us free will. We get to decide who we want to oversee our lives. Either Him or us.

I worked in prisons for 14 years. I have led hundreds of Alpha sessions. Alpha is run in churches, homes, and even prisons. It is a course on the basics of Christianity where a group comes together to socialize, listen to teaching, and get in smaller groups to discuss what was heard. I will sometimes ask the men gathered there, "Who's in charge of your life?" Someone will always proudly say, "I am!" To which my reply is, "How's that going?" There is usually a silence as the men realize that, since we are sitting in a prison, the answer is it's not really going very well. We are so proud of our independence. One of the most common songs played at funerals is Frank Sinatra's *I Did It My Way*. One of the main tenets of Satanism is self-worship. We think we are being independent. But someone is leading us. If it isn't God, all we really are is rebellious.

Even Jesus was under authority on earth. The Roman soldier understood this. He was a military man who stated, *"For I myself am a man under authority, with soldiers under me. I tell one to go, and he goes; and another to come, and he comes. I tell my servant to do something, and he does it"* (Matthew 8:9). Jesus was amazed at this faith, as he showed that he understood Jesus was clearly under authority because He had angels under his authority.

If we are to live lives from the Spirit, being influenced primarily from the throne room, we need to be under authority. I have decided to give the throne in my castle to God. I want Him to be the King of my castle. Then I know I'm safe under his authority, under his covering, his protection. and his provision.

There is a biblical precedence for this. In Revelation 4 we see the 24 elders around the throne of God:

They lay their crowns before the throne and say:
"You are worthy, our Lord and God,
*   to receive glory and honor and power,*
for you created all things,
*   and by your will they were created*
*   and have their being." (Revelation 4:10-11).*

So here comes one of those resistance verses I referred to earlier, but notice what comes before resistance:

Submit yourselves, then, to God. Resist the devil, and he will flee from you (James 4:7).

James is not saying, "Just say no!" He is saying, "Humble yourself before God, come under his authority. Then you can go into battle." If we are to fight giants, we need to take full responsibility and submit ourselves under legitimate authority.

David took full, personal responsibility to fight Goliath, and then he was sent by the authority of King Saul. David said to Saul, *"Let no one lose heart on account of this Philistine; your servant will go and fight him." Saul said to David, "Go, and the LORD be with you."* (1 Samuel 17:32,37).

If we decide to align our hearts with God's heart, our minds with his mind, our emotions with his emotions, our will with his will, then his power, love, and authority will flow from the throne room into the rest of our castle, and from there into the world. This is the first step to slay our giants and march sin out of our lives. We make God the King of our castle!

Having established that Jesus was on the throne of my castle, I began to exercise my spirit. I found that even

This is the first step to slay our giants and march sin out of our lives. We make God the King of our castle!

though my spirit was sealed with God's, I still needed to exercise my spirit and use the spiritual gifts I had been given. I started speaking in tongues—a lot. I would start my day with 20 minutes praying in the Spirit.

Speaking in tongues, or "praying in the spirit," is prophesied by Jesus and encouraged by Paul. Jesus said in Mark 16:17, *"And these signs will accompany those who believe: In my name they will drive out demons; they will speak in new tongues…"* Paul said, *"Pray in the Spirit at all times and on every occasion."* And, *"I thank God that I speak in tongues more than all of you"* (Ephesians 6:18, 1 Corinthians 14:18).

I first heard people singing in tongues on the day I came to faith in the chapel. Later I asked some of them about it. They just said it was easy and started speaking in tongues. Later that night I lay in bed and imitated what I had heard. Suddenly I realized I too was speaking in tongues. It was wonderful. It felt like my spirit had a complete language I could speak to God in. I can start it and stop it at any time. Sometimes if I'm driving or on a long walk, I pray in tongues the whole way. Other times I just find myself praying this way without even thinking about it. When I pray in tongues, it's the Spirit of God speaking through me. It's the Spirit speaking from the throne room into my heart.

We are encouraged by Paul to live by the Spirit, not by the flesh. I love to pray in the Spirit. God's Spirit does not fear or doubt. He doesn't know defeat. When we pray in the Spirit, He releases heaven's power into our lives. The enemy has NO DEFENSE against praying in tongues. It is God Himself speaking to the spiritual realm. I love this unfair advantage.

If we have the courage to put God in charge, things will change. In Proverbs, it says: *He becomes your personal bodyguard as you follow his ways, protecting and guarding you as you choose what is right* (Proverbs 2:7-8 TPT). What a wonderful promise. I watched this scripture come to pass in my life. If we want our castles back, we need to put someone in charge who knows how to run things and who will come alongside us to protect us and train us to do the right things.

I had to ask Jesus to be the King of my castle, and then surrender all control—and the results were amazing. God started to change things in my life. As my heart, mind, will, and emotions began to align with God's governance, my circumstances radically improved, and in many different areas, which surprised me! We started, very quickly, to come out of financial debt.

John writes us in 3 John 2: *"Beloved friend, I pray that you are prospering in every way and that you continually enjoy good health, just as your soul is prospering."* Where we had been struggling for years in constant debt, suddenly the situation changed and we were able to pay off several debts in a short period.

My health also improved. I had been afflicted with severe tension headaches for all my adult life. But now I realized that as I brought my life into line with God's words, it released healing to my body. The headaches began to reduce in frequency and severity. The words in Proverbs 4 came alive:

Listen carefully, my dear child, to everything that I teach you,
and pay attention to all that I have to say.
Fill your thoughts with my words
 until they penetrate deep into your spirit.
Then, as you unwrap my words,
 they will impart true life and radiant health
 into the very core of your being.
So above all, guard the affections of your heart,
for they affect all that you are (Proverbs 4: 20-23 TPT).

Question

Are you ready to make Him the King of your castle?

Prayer

Father God, this day I take full responsibility for my actions. I decide to live under your authority. I lay my crown down at your feet and ask You to take the throne in my castle. You are my Lord. You are the King of my castle. Lead me, Lord. Teach me to live by the Spirit. Teach me to hear and obey your voice. Cover me, Lord. Heal me. Grow me. Protect me, provide for me, Lord. Give me your faith, give me your courage. Send me out in the power of your name to destroy the works of the enemy in my castle and beyond.

(John 15:14, Romans 8:9, Revelation 4:10, Luke 10:9).

10

RECLAIM YOUR HEART

MANY OF THE CONVERSATIONS I hear about "slaying our giants" are about our circumstances—things that have happened to us, like debt, marriage difficulties, infertility, health issues. But where addiction is concerned, the culprit hasn't come from the outside. We have allowed a giant into our hearts. We have let it operate on the inside of us.

This was made clear to me when I realized I had been "dancing with a giant" instead of slaying it. In fact, we'd been doing the rumba together for quite a few years. I had not been fully resisting it. At times, I had actually been resisting God. Everything was backwards.

My heart had become divided, compartmentalized, hardened. My conscience had become blunted. I was full of inner conflict.

For this people's heart has become calloused;
they hardly hear with their ears,
and they have closed their eyes.
Otherwise they might see with their eyes,

hear with their ears,
understand with their hearts
and turn, and I would heal them (Matthew 13:15).

God Will Help Us

The good news is that God longs to heal us. We have to grasp that fact. Let it sink in. It's what He is dying to do for us. If we have asked God to be on the throne and are submitting to his leadership and authority, He *will* reclaim our hearts. It is what He does. Do a word search for "heart" in the Bible and you can read all 725 references. God is after our hearts from the beginning to the end of the story.

I will sprinkle clean water on you, and you will be clean; I will cleanse you from all your impurities and from all your idols. I will give you a new heart and put a new spirit in you; I will remove from you your heart of stone and give you a heart of flesh. And I will put my Spirit in you and move you to follow my decrees and be careful to keep my laws. Then you will live in the land I gave your ancestors; you will be my people, and I will be your God. I will save you from all your uncleanness (Ezekiel 36:24-29).

God wants to help us by softening our hardened hearts with his Spirit, like water on dry ground. By putting his Spirit in us, we will not have to try to follow his decrees; we will want to follow Him because we love Him. When we purposefully invite God to live in our hearts, He starts to change us. He takes away old desires and gives us new desires that are aligned with his heart.

God wants our hearts to be clean and aligned with his. God wants the giants slayed. The second we start praying this way, He steps in and helps us because we are going in his name. As David told Goliath, *"You come against me with sword and spear and javelin, but I come against you in the name of the Lord Almighty..."* (1 Sam 17:45).

Question

Do you believe God wants you to defeat your giants?

Fight In the Light

I remember when I was doing martial arts training at school, a friend and I decided that, to train our senses, it would be a good idea to spar with the lights out in the gym. We were young. I think we were trying to become some sort of ninja-level fighters. It was completely dark, like pitch black. It was a really bad idea. Either we were too far away from each other, flailing away at the air, or when we got close enough for contact, we were hitting each other full force without being able to defend. It hurt. We soon stopped. Fighting in the dark is a bad idea.

Light dispels darkness. You don't have to tell the darkness to leave in a dark room—just turn on the light and it goes. Same with our personal battles we've kept hidden for so long—when we shine a light on them, they tend to scatter like cockroaches. Although it isn't easy—and nothing worth having ever is—it has been worth it. I have learned to be transparent on my journey by being honest about my struggles along the way with close, trusted loved ones. Fortunately I have been blessed with close friends and a wonderful wife with whom I can share these things. This kind of revelation is obviously painful for a spouse to hear. But it's not as bad as the constant dull pain of living with a person who has a divided heart and is not fully committed to the relationship. When I partner with my spouse for healing, when we are praying for each other during this process, it accelerates the journey to freedom and results in a stronger bond than ever.

During the crisis I referred to earlier, God was giving me dreams. Soon after I was given the picture of dancing with the giant who had both my hands in an interlinked "stronghold," I had another dream. I dreamt I was in church listening to a great teacher. I felt the Holy Spirit on me and noticed a friend of mine sitting next to me, holding my hand in the same interlinked way as the giant had held my hands. But it was supportive and caring. When I woke up, I had one thought: "You can't hold hands with two people at once." I could either hold hands with supportive friends, or with the giant—but not both.

Question

Who can you share this journey with?

In Psalm 36:9 it says, *"in your light we see light."* As soon as we bring something into the light, we see it for what it is and God gives us further revelation.

As I brought my condition into the light, it led me to a place of real repentance. God started to reveal more and more truth about my situation and what I had let into my castle. I now saw that even seemingly innocent actions—like watching a a certain TV channel or glancing at a social media post—had been invitations to the Devil to take up residence and bring more demons with him. I became aware of how I had relaxed my boundaries, opening the gate to the enemy with little concern for the consequences.

There's a transformation that God initiates when we truly turn to Him. He begins to sharpen our conscience. I have seen this working in prisons. Men who had done so much bad stuff for so long that their consciences had become all but useless as a moral guide began to feel bad for the things they had done as God began to draw close to them. This is the work of the Holy Spirit as He begins to hone our consciences back to life.

This realization of where I had been brought me deep sadness. I often found myself on my knees, asking God to be the King of my life again. I realized I had let things into my soul and into my heart that should never have been there. I had hardened my heart to God as a result. I would pray for Him to soften my heart by his Spirit—and He did. Like water on hard ground, He pours his love into our hearts by his Spirit (Romans 6:6).

This was a different sorrow to the kind I used to feel when I had sinned. That was really self-pity; I was sad I had gone off track, again. Sad for myself that I had failed. But it didn't necessarily lead to any change. It was "worldly sorrow," not "godly sorrow." Paul is glad for the Corinthians, *"yet now I am happy, not because you were made sorry, but because your sorrow led you to repentance"* (2 Corinthians 7:9).

As I asked Him to cleanse my heart, He did. I found my joy returning. It was only when I began to experience joy again that I realized I had gradually lost the joy of the Lord over the years. I fell in love with my wife again. It was amazing.

Question

How do you feel about the things you've been doing in private? Is there anything you've been hiding from others?

In prayer, we can give God access to your whole heart.

Prayer

Lord, I give you my heart today. Please come and fill my heart with your love by your Holy Spirit. Give me an undivided heart. Purify my heart, Lord. Wash through me and fill my heart with your desires. Forgive me, Lord, where I have given affection to things that should never have been in my heart. May I always turn my heart to the throne room and away from the world. May you be the greatest influence on my heart every day. I love you, Lord.

Amen.

(Psalm 51, Romans 5:5, Deuteronomy 6:5).

Keep Your Eyes on the Prize

David was keen to hear what his reward would be for defeating the giant Philistine. He asked twice what would be given to the one who killed the giant. Let us keep our eyes on the prize, like David did. When we defeat this enemy, we will:

- Get our hearts back, undivided, free of inner conflict, sensitive to God
- Get our spouse's heart back (either present or future if you are not married)
- Get our authority back
- Get our identity back

If that sounds good, keep it in mind when we go to battle for our castles. Addiction takes up so much energy. Instead of actively fighting our giants, we're usually just trying to get through the day. We're fighting from a weakened position because of our divided hearts and having ourselves on the throne, not God. But once we have established our true identities and our hearts are right with God, we can fight from an incredibly strong position with all the resources of God at our disposal. Now we are fighting with the authority of the King and with his power. Now we have formidable backup!

Go on the Offensive

An offensive is a military operation that seeks, through an aggressive action of armed forces to occupy territory, to gain an objective, or achieve some larger strategic goal.

Just as Jesus went on the attack in the temple, there are times when only an attack on the enemy will work for us. He is on *our* turf; he is in *our* castle. This is not the time to defend. This is not the time to negotiate. This is time to go on the offensive to drive out the giant from the keep, across the grounds and out the gates. This is time to attack.

For years as a young Christian, I didn't know that God's word, in itself, has power. I had simply not been around the kind of Christians who used God's word as a weapon as the Bible tells us to in Ephesians 6:17: *Take the helmet of salvation and the sword of the Spirit, which is the word of God.* I now use God's words in prayer to defeat and defend myself against the enemy's tactics. I would be foolish not to use this powerful weapon at my disposal! The prayers in this book are not just my thoughts, they are based on scripture—on the word of God. They are our sword.

Say this out loud. It is a decree. It needs to be heard—by you, by the enemy, by God, and by the angels who are "ministering spirits" fighting for you.

Declaration

I am speaking to sin. I come to you in the authority of Jesus Christ who lives in me and is greater than anything that is in the world. I resist you and stand firm in the faith of Christ. No weapon you use against me will prosper. I condemn any word of accusation sent against me. I have the victory in this battle because I am in Christ, who is victorious in all things. You are a defeated enemy because Jesus nailed you to the cross and made a public spectacle of you. I command you to leave now and never to return. In the name of Jesus. (Luke 10:19, 1 John 4:4, James 4:6, 1 Peter 5:8, Isaiah 54:17, 1 Corinthians 15:57, Collosians 2:15).

Filling Our Hearts

It wasn't enough just to be pruned of negative things. Having asked God to clean my heart, I needed to fill the void with good things. I began to listen to instrumental worship music when I was working, praying or just hanging out. I stopped watching TV so much and spent more time being creative. I began to consciously avoid things I knew were not helpful for me. I began to guard my heart.

Solomon tells us: *So above all, guard the affections of your heart, for they affect all that you are. Pay attention to the welfare of your innermost being, for from there flows the wellspring of life* (Proverbs 4:23 TPT).

Paul tells us in Philippians 4:8: *Finally, brothers and sisters, whatever is true, whatever is noble, whatever is right, whatever is pure, whatever is lovely, whatever is admirable—if anything is excellent or praiseworthy—think about such things.*

My wife and I began to have real, vulnerable conversations every day about our hearts. When I became stressed or angry (which became less often), I consciously turned my heart toward the throne room—and not to the world—for guidance, reassurance and comfort. I began to look to the spirit, and not to the flesh. It changed everything. The inner conflict subsided and I began to find life and peace.

It's really important when we want to stop doing something that we start doing something else to replace it. Developing good habits is vital in the process of restoration from addictive behavior. Jesus warns us in Matthew 12 what happens when a demon is removed and the "house" it came out of is left empty:

When an impure spirit comes out of a person, it goes through arid places seeking rest and does not find it. Then it says, "I will return to the house I left." When it arrives, it finds the house unoccupied, swept clean and put in order. Then it goes and takes with it seven other spirits more wicked than itself, and they go in and live there. And the final condition of that person is worse than the first (Matthew 12: 43:45).

I was learning to fill my heart with God's word and spirit. The next step was to dismantle the strongholds I had built. I would start by renewing my thinking.

11

RENEW YOUR MIND

MY THOUGHTS HAD BECOME DISTORTED. I had constructed ways of thinking that had actually defended sin in my life. I had created neural pathways that ingrained unhealthy ways of reacting and responding to adverse circumstances. However, once God had become the King of my castle and my heart was given back to Him, I could really set about renewing my mind. This is probably the part of the process that requires the most work and takes the longest. It is worth saying here that the entire process of reclaiming my castle took time and required planning and effort. Even though God was the doing the heavy lifting once I asked Him to take the seat of power, I still needed to cooperate and give Him space to operate in my life. It has taken time for me to learn to think in certain ways and this is an ongoing process.

I began to read the Bible daily. I not only read it, I would meditate on it, write about it and ask God what He was teaching me through it. Just reading was not enough. It's when I meditated and thought about a passage, or even a verse, that I begin to learn. As I digested the word of God, it became part of me. Ezekiel was told by God, *"Son of man, eat this scroll I am giving you and fill your stomach with it." So I ate it, and it tasted as sweet as honey in my mouth"* (Ezekiel 3.3).

I began to devour the Bible. I began to write letters from God to me—imagining what He was saying to me. They were full of scripture, and again and again He told me He loved me, washing my heart, renewing my mind.

My heart changed very quickly; my mind took longer. I remember back to the day in the chapel when I first asked God into my life. I was 27 years old. I had come to a place in my life where I no longer trusted anyone, including myself. I was desperate to find the truth, and to my amazement, I found it—not in books or philosophy, but in a person. Jesus said, "I am the truth..." That day I asked him into my life and He came in. It was a very physical experience.

He flooded my heart with his Holy Spirit. I fell to the floor on my knees and wept. Immediately I felt an overwhelming love for God and for people that I had never experienced before. My heart was transformed in a minute. I was born again in that moment. But my IQ hadn't changed. I had experienced an event. The renewing of my mind is much more of a process. Paul tells us in Romans 12:2 to *"be transformed by the renewing our minds,"* but how do we do that?

The enemy gets into the castle by deceiving you. At some point you have believed a lie, usually about yourself or about God. (In the next chapter we'll take a look at some of the most common lies.) These lies become the foundations of a stronghold. What I've come to realize is that behind every inner battle is a root lie. Until you identify that lie and counter it with the truth, you'll continue to fight the same battle over and over.

Renewing your mind involves demolishing any strongholds that have set themselves up in opposition to the truth. It involves exposing root lies—then taking an axe to that root.

Only light can dispel darkness (John 12:46). Only truth can displace lies, and the truth will set us free (John 8:23).

Mounting this inner offensive takes guts. It is not for the faint of heart. Many a man has walked away from this battle. But you, my friend, have the courage of a knight who is capable of fighting darkness and lies, because you are on a mission from the King. Your face is set like flint. You now have the power and authority to destroy the strongholds in your life. It's time to clear out the darkness by bringing light. It's time to take your sword of the spirit, which is the word of God and take captive the lies that have been dominating the castle.

For though we live in the world, we do not wage war as the world does. The weapons we fight with are not the weapons of the world. On the contrary, they have divine power to demolish strongholds. We demolish arguments and every pretension that sets itself up against the knowledge of God, and we take captive every thought to make it obedient to Christ (2 Corinthians 10: 3-5).

Dismantle the Strongholds

For me, one of the biggest lies I believed was that I would never be free of addictive behavior because I was a "sinner."

A few years ago, I remember walking around my garden saying, "God, I am just a sinful man." I felt God slap me around the face and clearly heard Him in my spirit say, *Stop saying that about yourself!* It was so real I was shocked, but it sent me on a quest to find the truth about my identity. I had been told repeatedly in church that I am a sinner. If I'm not a sinner, then what am I?

How had that lie become so engrained in my thinking? One way the enemy tricks us is to take scriptures about sin out of context and use them to get us to come to a false conclusion and agree with a lie, usually concerning our core identity. It's just a slight variation from the truth, so it's a subtle deception. In other words, it sounds about right. Some church leaders have fallen prey to these nuanced misstatements of truth, too, and have unwittingly peddled lies to us and damaged our hearts in the process.

Here's a classic example of this subtle truth-twisting scheme of Satan. Romans 3:23 says: ...*for all have sinned and fall short of the glory of God.*

This scripture oftentimes is (mis)used to support the claim that we are all sinners. How many times have you heard that you are a wretched sinner? The false conclusion is made by confusing the verb for a noun—it takes something we *do* (sin) and claims it is something we *are* (a sinner). We need to get this right—Paul is not suggesting our core identity is a sinner. Looked at in context, he's talking to the Jewish believers who thought that because they had the "law," they were better than the Gentiles. He's explaining that a righteousness from God apart from the law has been made known. It's not about sin; it's about attaining righteousness. It's about how we're all justified by faith in Jesus.

The enemy will take these scriptures and get you to pin your very identity on them. "I'm just a sinner (saved by grace)." We wallow in that identity and the place of defeat it represents. No, I'm not saying we never sin. Of course, we do. But if we do, we have an advocate—we confess and we move on. What we don't do is believe this is who we are. That is a lie.

So, what is the truth that will dismantle this lie? What is the light that will dispel the darkness?

The truth is, Jesus came to deal with our sin and give us a new identity.

John the baptist announces Jesus by saying, *"Look! The Lamb of God who takes away the sin of the world!"* (John 1:29)

The truth is that He... *appeared so that he might take away our sins. And in him is no sin. No one who lives in him keeps on sinning* (1 John 3: 5-6).

The truth is that ...*God made him who had no sin to be sin for us, so that in him we might become the righteousness of God* (2 Corinthians 5:21).

The truth is that … *his divine power has given us everything we need for life and godliness through our knowledge of him who called us by his own glory and goodness* (1 Peter 3).

Notice that all these truths are about Jesus, and we are in Him. We can live lives of godliness that are not dominated by sin.

Romans 6 tells us the truth about our new identity. We died with Christ. When He died, our old self also died. This is a truth we must grasp. The old man is dead and buried; he is no more. We will not *feel* this because it happened to our spirit. We must know it: *For we know that our old self was crucified with him so that the body ruled by sin might be done away with, that we should no longer be slaves to sin because anyone who has died has been set free from sin* (Romans 6:6-7). If this passage is true, how can I say I've died to sin yet my core identity is a sinner? It doesn't make sense—it's a lie.

Romans 7 is often used to justify continual personal sin and to explain the fact that we're still sinners. I'm convinced it is widely misinterpreted. The subheading in the NIV, *"Struggling with sin"* (not in the original text) is very misleading. The passage is not about struggling with sin. Looking at the context, Romans 7:14-25 is about what happens when we try to live under the law. Paul here talks about the effects of trying to obey command-ments without Christ living in us. I try as hard as I can, but without Christ, I fail. But Romans 6 and 8 tell us we have Christ living in us and this means we *can* live lives of godliness, not dominated by sin. If we read Romans 7 as a description of our continual current position, then

Romans 6 and Romans 8 make little sense. It must be read in context.

Romans 8 tells us we have been set free from the law of "sin and death;" that we can have minds that are set on what the Spirit of God desires; that we can have a mind controlled by life and peace; that our spirit is alive because of his righteousness in us; that we have a spirit of sonship in us; that because He lives in us, we are children of God. This is our true identity.

Knowing this, why then would we say, "I am just a sinner"? It's a lie we've believed about ourselves. It is a stronghold in our lives that creates shadows where sin can continue to operate. The truth is that because the spirit of God lives in us, we are the place where God has chosen to demonstrate his righteousness. We are his habitation. You are his son or daughter, beloved of the Father, empowered by the spirit, imitating Christ and united with Him, going to battle against sin.

Question

Are you recognizing any lies you've believed about God or yourself? If not, can you ask God to reveal any lies to you?

Prayer

Lord, in your light we see light. I thank You that we have the mind of Christ. Give me more revelation about my thinking. Expose my blind spots, Lord. Show me when I'm believing lies about You and about

myself. Show me when I'm thinking impure or unloving thoughts.
Lord, give me your wisdom. Teach me your ways, Lord, and show me
things I do not know.
(Psalm 36:9, John 8:44, Isaiah 55:7, Proverbs 8:17,
1 Corinthians 2:16, Jeremiah 33:3).

Taking Captives in the Castle

There will be ongoing skirmishes in the castle. Evil
thoughts will still run through the grounds. But now, any
thought that's contrary to God's word is to be exposed
and dealt with. It is to be brought before the King. Any
thought that sows doubt about who God is, any thought
that brings fear, any thought that questions who we are in
God, any temptation to sin is from the Devil.

How do you know if a thought is true? Well, we can only
know this if we have the truth in us. We only have the
truth in us if we know God's truth. His truth is in his word.
If we fill our minds and hearts with his word, we'll be able
to know if a thought is true, pure, and loving. Jesus said,
"…the words that I speak unto you, they are spirit, and they are life"
(John 6:63). He also said, *"I am the way, the truth and the life"*
(John 14:6). The more familiar we are with his words, the
easier it will be to spot thoughts that are not in alignment
with his. Proverbs tells us, *Train your heart to listen when I speak*
and open your spirit wide to expand your discernment… (Proverbs
2:2 TPT). The Spirit of God is living within us, in our
throne room, speaking to our spirits, to our hearts, and to
our mind, will, and emotions.

Once we have the truth in us, there's a way to test these thoughts that come to our minds. We can ask these questions:

Is it true?

Is it pure?

Is it loving?

Is it giving good fruit?

If the answer is no, if the answer brings shame or condemnation rather than encouragement and life, then we have identified a lie. Great, so, once we recognize an imposter in the castle grounds, what do we do? Well, the Bible tells us clearly: Any thought that is trying to build an argument or mislead us about who God is and who we are is to be taken captive.

We tear down arguments and every presumption set up against the knowledge of God; and we take captive every thought to make it obedient to Christ (2 Cor 10:5).

When I get a wicked thought in my mind, I don't entertain it. I don't mull it over and examine it; I don't wallow in it or try to ignore it. I am quick to recognize it does not align with God's word. I imagine myself dragging it by the scruff of the neck and throwing it down at the foot of a cross. I take it to the King and make it obedient.

"Here, Lord, take this thing!"

Decree

Lord, I will ruthlessly pursue the truth. I will speak the truth about you and about myself. I refuse to believe the lies the enemy has told me. I will renew my mind with your word and use the sword of the spirit, which is the word of God, to demolish ungodly arguments and pretensions that have set themselves up in my castle in opposition to the knowledge of God. I will take every ungodly thought captive and throw it down at the cross to make it obedient to you. In the name of Jesus. Amen.

(John 6:63, John 8:32, John 14:6, Romans 12:2, Ephesians 6:17, 2 Corinthians 10:3-4).

Dear brothers and sisters, let us courageously pursue and maintain truth so we will be set free from the lies that have bound us. Let us take in the word of God so we will know the truth and we can destroy the strongholds that have been built in our castles. Let us live in the light of Christ, in obedience to the King, so that there are no longer deep inner conflicts in our hearts. Let us renew our minds and gain our integrity once more so we can live lives of godliness, honor, and peace.

12

RESTORE YOUR SOUL

The Will

THERE IS NOTHING WRONG WITH the human will. It's designed to be the most obstinate thing on the face of the earth. If you doubt me, try taking on a three-year-old who is refusing to do what you tell them. You will find out just how fully formed and highly functioning the will of even a partly formed human can be.

God created our will to defy everything that comes against it and to persevere in the face of relentless opposition. When functioning in line with God, it is our will that brings his will on earth. It helps us make the right decisions. It helps us act in a disciplined manner.

The trouble is that if our will is compromised too often, it becomes emaciated and weak. Instead of standing guard over our gates, deciding what does and does not come in, it becomes ineffective, like a beggar leaning on the doorpost instead of a guard in full armor standing at the threshold of our soul.

Our will should be used to make good choices. God makes this clear to the Israelite community in the desert:

This day I call the heavens and the earth as witnesses against you that I have set before you life and death, blessings and curses. Now choose life, so that you and your children may live and that you may love the LORD your God, listen to his voice, and hold fast to him (Deuteronomy 30:19).

So how do we make good decisions if our will (decision maker) has become emaciated and misused? What we need is wisdom.

You may think, *I'm smart. I know a lot. I have knowledge.* Yet wisdom is not just knowledge; it is that and so much more. You can have knowledge without wisdom. Wisdom is the ability to use knowledge correctly. It's revelation, insight, experience, and intuition combined with what we know. If we have wisdom, we will make good decisions based on our knowledge.

James tells us, *"If any of you lacks wisdom, you should ask God, who gives generously to all without finding fault, and it will be given to you"* (James 1:5).

There is a storehouse of wisdom available to all of us. If we turn to the "book of wisdom" in the Bible, we will find what we're looking for. In Proverbs 2:8 it says:

For the Lord has a hidden storehouse of wisdom made accessible to his godly ones. He becomes your personal bodyguard as you follow his ways, protecting and guarding you as you choose what is right (TPT).

If we make God the King of our castles, He will show us the way to the hidden storehouse of wisdom. It is accessible to his godly ones, yet it is hidden from the ungodly. Jesus told his disciples that *"…the knowledge of the secrets of the kingdom of heaven has been given to you, but not to them"* (Matthew 13:11). Not only will we find wisdom and, in doing so, gain the ability to make good decisions, but God will become our personal bodyguard as we follow his ways. This is one of the amazing things God does

> *If we make God the King of our castles, He will show us the way to the hidden storehouse of wisdom.*

when He takes the throne of our lives. It's as if He comes to join us taking control of the gates so we can learn to do it ourselves. It's as if we have a strong, well-armed, experienced soldier alongside the gatekeeper of the castle. Our weakened will is being retrained to guard our gates.

As the lies are exposed and the strongholds dismantled, the shadows disappear and we learn to see the deceptions for what they are: attempts by sin to enter the castle. Then with God training us, we can firmly close the gates. Solomon goes on to explain what happens when we get wisdom:

Then you will discover all that is just, proper, and fair, and be empowered to make the right decisions as you walk into your destiny. When wisdom wins your heart and revelation breaks in, true pleasure enters your soul. If you choose to follow good counsel, divine design will watch over you and understanding will protect you from making poor choices. It will rescue you from evil in disguise and from those who speak duplicities (Proverbs 2:7-12 TPT).

Once our spirit, mind, and will are turning to God and aligned with his will, his power is released in our lives. Prayers are answered. Inner conflict diminishes. And the peace, love, and joy of God begin to manifest in our lives to those around us.

Decree

I will walk with you in complete freedom, for I seek to follow your every command.
When I stand before kings, I will tell them the truth and will never be ashamed.
My passion and delight is in your word, for I love what you say to me!
I long for more revelation of your truth, for I love the light of your word as I meditate on your decrees.
Amen. (Psalm 119:45-48).

The Emotions

God is Spirit. His Spirit speaks directly to our spirit. When we are born again our spirit is immediately made perfect and is joined with his Spirit. We are sealed in Christ. We still need to do spiritual exercises to learn to live by the spirit. And we still need to renew our minds by bringing our thinking into line with God's word. We must exercise our will to align with his will. And we must turn our emotions to God and not to the world for healing and comfort.

We have become a feeling-based culture. It's part of the demonic plan to keep us in the flesh and keep us out of the Spirit. The world, the flesh, and the Devil all want us to be led by our feelings. In this way we remain in captivity to the "lusts of the flesh." At the same time these forces want to keep us away from the truth, darkening our understanding of God.

I don't want to be susceptible to these watered-down, worldly ways; neither does God want that for us. He wants us to gain knowledge so we can stand our ground. Paul repeatedly challenges us throughout his letters to "know." Just one example is in Romans 6:

*"Or don't you **know** that all of us who were baptised into Christ Jesus were baptised into his death?"*

*"For we **know** that our old self was crucified with him so that the body ruled by sin might be done away with, that we should no longer be slaves to sin..."*

*"For we **know** that since Christ was raised from the dead, he cannot die again; death no longer has mastery over him."*

*"Don't you **know** that when you offer yourselves to someone as obedient slaves, you are slaves of the one you obey—whether you are slaves to sin, which leads to death, or to obedience, which leads to righteousness?* (Romans 6:3, 6, 9, 16).

Notice there's no indication we should "feel" these things. In fact, in the New Testament, the word *feel* appears a total of just four times. The words *know*, or *knowledge*, appear over 400 times. This should give us a clue about God's priorities concerning feelings and knowledge.

When our emotions come into line with his heart, this looks like compassion. When Jesus showed emotion, He was moved by compassion for those in need around Him. His emotions reflected God's, passionately defending the things of God and showing loving kindness to the people He came in contact with.

We won't always *feel* our relationship with God. If we rely on our feelings, we won't see the truth. We need to *know* what our true relationship with God is. If we trust Him, He will step in and help us. If we turn to Him for comfort when we're hurting emotionally, He will put a guard around us.

Never worry about anything. But in every situation let God know what you need in prayers and requests while giving thanks. Then God's peace, which goes beyond anything we can imagine, will guard your thoughts and emotions through Christ Jesus (Philippians 4:6-8 GW).

My prayer for us is this, from Ephesians 6:17-19:

*I keep asking that the God of our Lord Jesus Christ, the glorious Father, may give you the Spirit of wisdom and revelation, so that you may **know** him better. I pray that the eyes of your heart may be enlightened in order that you may **know** the hope to which he has called you, the riches of his glorious inheritance in his holy people, and his incomparably great power for us who believe.*

Question

Do you tend to base your life mostly on your feelings or on knowledge and wisdom?

13

STRENGTHEN THE BODY

The five senses of the body form the gates to our castle, according to John Bunyan in his book *The Holy War*, as previously mentioned. These are the Eye-gate, Ear-gate, Mouth-gate, Nose-gate, and Skin-gate.

If someone came to your door one night and said, "Hi, I'd like to come in and entertain you tonight." You would probably ask what kind of entertainment they're offering (or immediately slam the door in their face).

"Well, it includes sex, violence, foul language, sexual violence and adult themes."

Would you let them in? I would send him packing. But we casually let these things in all the time when we watch TV and films. I went to watch a movie recently and this list above came up on screen at the beginning. I asked myself, *Do I want to let these things into my castle, at the risk they'll get into my heart?* The answer was no, so I switched to something else. I was guarding my heart. In any circumstance where

I have control over what comes into my castle, I will exercise my ability to control it.

I have internet filters on my phone and computer that report to my wife by email every week. It even takes screenshots of anything that looks like it could be pornographic. These only work, however, if the enemy has been flushed out of the castle. (Just a few years ago it would not have worked for me; but I had already done the tough work.) The gates in a castle don't have handles on the outside; they can only be opened from within. How I use my senses to let stuff in or keep stuff out of my castle is up to me.

Be Careful What You Expose Yourself To

Proverbs gives us fair warning about exposing ourselves to harmful influences and allowing ourselves to be enticed by sin. Read this passage and see how many of the young man's senses are being used to entice him:

Looking out the window of my house one day
I noticed among the mindless crowd
    a simple, naïve young man who was about to go astray.
There he was, walking down the street.
    Then he turned the corner,
    going on his way hurrying to the house of the harlot—
    the woman he had planned to meet.
There he was in the twilight as darkness fell,
    convinced no one was watching
    as he entered the black shadows of hell.

That's when their rendezvous began.
   A woman of the night appeared,
   dressed to kill the strength of any man.
   She was decked out as a harlot, pursuing her amorous plan.
Her voice was seductive, rebellious, and boisterous
   as she wandered far from what's right.
Her type can be found soliciting on street corners
   on just about any night.
She wrapped her arms around the senseless young man
   and held him tight—
   she enticed him with kisses that seemed so right.
   Then, with insolence, she whispered in his ear,
"Come with me. It'll be all right.
   I've got everything we need for a feast.
   I'll cook you a wonderful dinner
   So here I am—I'm all yours!
You're the very one I've looked for,
   the one I knew I wanted from the moment I saw you.
   That's why I've come out here tonight,
   so I could meet a man just like you.
 I've spread my canopy bed with coverings,
   lovely multicolored Egyptian linens
   ready for you to lie down on.
I've sprinkled the sheets with intoxicating perfume
   made from myrrh, aloes, and sweet cinnamon.
Come, let's get comfortable and take pleasure in each other
   and make love all night!
There's no one home, for my husband's away on business...

(Proverbs 7: 6-10, 21-23 TPT).

She uses every sense to seduce the naïve young man. She knocks at every gate of his castle—she dresses to allure his eyes, touches and kisses him, she has perfumed her bed, promises food for his taste, and assaults his ears with her seductive words. She employs every trick of the enemy to get him to let sin into his castle.

14

THE CASTLE DEFENDED

OUR CASTLES ARE THE MOST sophisticated defense systems ever invented. They are perfectly designed to repel invasions and to discern deception. We have impregnable walls, impenetrable gates, an astonishing intelligence network, highly functioning emotions, iron-like gatekeeper wills, hearts that are wonderfully and fearfully made, and spirits that are in intimate relationship with God Himself. The question is how to use it all. The key is who is in control. The really big question is: Who is the king of our castle?

If we make God the King of our castle, we have God living within us. His Holy Spirit dwells inside our bodies. Paul puts it this way:

Have you forgotten that your body is now the sacred temple of the Spirit of Holiness, who lives in you? You don't belong to yourself any longer, for the gift of God, the Holy Spirit, lives inside your sanctuary. You were God's expensive purchase, paid for with tears of blood, so by all means, then, use your body to bring glory to God! (1 Corinthians 6:19-20).

We have the most wonderful bodies. God has given us everything we need to defend ourselves if we use them for his glory. Again, the question is: Who or what is in control of our bodies?

Paul reminds us that, now that we have Jesus on the throne, sin can no longer rule over us:

Sin is a dethroned monarch; so you must no longer give it an opportunity to rule over your life, controlling how you live and compelling you to obey its desires and cravings. So then, refuse to answer its call to surrender your body as a tool for wickedness. Instead, passionately answer God's call to keep yielding your body to him as one who has now experienced resurrection life! You live now for his pleasure, ready to be used for his noble purpose. Remember this: sin will not conquer you, for God already has! You are not governed by law but governed by the reign of the grace of God (Romans 6: 12-14 TPT).

Question

Are you convinced that you don't have to obey sin anymore?

Prayer

Lord, I dedicate my body to you today. I am a temple or your Holy Spirit. My body was paid for by Jesus on the cross. Sin will no longer master me, as you are my master. Lord, lead me today, give me revelation to see when I am under attack and to always act with wisdom. Remind me that sin cannot rule over me because you are on the throne of my castle. Above all else, may my mind, will and emotions guard my heart and may I turn to you for leadership, guidance, love and comfort. Amen.

(1 Corinthians 6:19-20, Romans 6:14, Proverbs 4:23).

15

THE CASTLE RESTORED

A CASTLE CAN ONLY BE restored from the inside out. We have to first and foremost establish Jesus as the King of our castles. When we do this, extraordinary changes take place. We have the full force of heaven operating in our favor. God Himself takes control and begins to wash our hearts and sharpen our consciences. Our minds are renewed as we engage with his word, and his Holy Spirit brings revelation to the truth. Our wills are trained by his, coming alongside us to help us make good decisions. Our emotions begin to heal and come into line with his and our compassion for others increases.

I said at the beginning of this book that God has a plan for our lives. I believe He wants us to be strong in Him and that our castles should be safe places for others to run to when they're vulnerable and under attack. A castle should not be a ruin but a place of refuge for the widows, the orphans, the lost. Our castles should be places of leadership and mercy, of sanctuary and provision where people feel safe once the castle gates are closed.

If we have the courage to take our castles back, to turn to God, to go to war against the sin that has gotten inside the walls, we will become a safe haven for others to run to. With the spirit of Jesus living in us, we will be able to say of ourselves the scripture He quoted when He began his ministry on earth:

The Spirit of the Sovereign LORD is on me,
because the LORD has anointed me
to proclaim good news to the poor.
He has sent me to bind up the brokenhearted,
to proclaim freedom for the captives
and release from darkness for the prisoners,
to proclaim the year of the LORD's favour
and the day of vengeance of our God,
to comfort all who mourn,
and provide for those who grieve in Zion—
to bestow on them a crown of beauty
instead of ashes,
the oil of joy
instead of mourning,
and a garment of praise
instead of a spirit of despair.
They will be called oaks of righteousness,
a planting of the LORD
for the display of his splendour.
They will rebuild the ancient ruins
and restore the places long devastated;
they will renew the ruined cities
that have been devastated for generations.
Strangers will shepherd your flocks;

foreigners will work your fields and vineyards.
And you will be called priests of the LORD,
*   you will be named ministers of our God.*
You will feed on the wealth of nations,
*   and in their riches you will boast.*
(Isaiah 61:1-6).

Courage for the Road to Restoration

A knight earns his title for service and devotion to protecting the castle in honor of the king. You are born of nobility. It is a high calling. This is your rightful place, under the lordship of your King. It begins with accepting your royal identity.

The journey of restoring yourself to full kingship under Jesus isn't easy—but it is worth it. It's a process; it takes time. I had to learn to be patient with myself while learning to be disciplined. I had to teach myself to continually turn to the Source of all life when I was under pressure. My relationships changed with those closest to me, especially with my wife as we learned to grow closer to each other again.

I made sure, above all else, to ask God to be the King of my castle every day and to spend time with Him. Today I am in a place where I need Him as much as I ever have. As men we often want to fix ourselves, so that we will never be tempted again. I have learned that if my castle walls are made up of stones, God is the mortar that fills the gaps and stops the structure from falling apart. I think He leaves us with vulnerabilities so that we will learn to be humble and dependent on Him. The aim is not to fix our flesh and to become independent, but to strengthen our spirit by being dependent on Him. This is true restoration—to an intimate relationship with the Father in the spirit.

I realized this task of restoration was not just for me. It was for my family, my community, and for others who found that their castles were in ruins. There was resistance. The enemy kept telling me, "If you let people know you've struggled with these things, it'll ruin your reputation." I just swung my sword at him—the word of God.

Instead of your shame
  you will receive a double portion,
and instead of disgrace
  you will rejoice in your inheritance.
And so you will inherit a double portion in your land,
  and everlasting joy will be yours (Isaiah 61:7).

If we choose this road, we will not suffer shame or disgrace, but will inherit a double portion and receive everlasting joy. I felt it was too important to remain quiet. Silencing us is, after all, one of the enemy's key strategies. Satan is terrified of Christians speaking the truth and he seeks to quash our voices with the threat of shame. Addiction has silenced the men in the church for too long. It has to end.

So, I chose to take courage and follow Jesus, who took all my sin and shame when He hung on the cross. I joined Him in his cause, to proclaim the Good News to the poor, to bind up the broken hearted and to set the captives free.

We can live with a higher calling on our lives. Our dreams can come alive again. We can become the men and women God had in his mind when He breathed life into us.

I will leave you with the words of the knight's code from the medieval epic poem, Song of Roland, written in the eighth century:

Fear God
Maintain his church
Speak the truth at all times
Protect the weak and defenseless
Care for widows and orphans
Respect and honor women
Obey those in authority
Fight your enemies fearlessly

If we take up this challenge, I believe we will not only take back our castles, but we can become men and women who, having established places of protection and sanctuary, then go on to take back his Kingdom.

But that, my friends, is another story.

Daily Prayer

Lord, I thank you that you conceived me and have loved me since the beginning of time. You sent your Son Jesus to rescue me from sin and death. I am your precious child. I thank you that you have saved me. You have a plan for my life. I reject any identity that the enemy has put on me. I am fearfully and wonderfully made. This day I commit to see myself and to speak of myself as a son (or daughter) of the Most High King. Establish my identity in you, Lord.

Father God, this day I take full responsibility for my actions. I decide to live under your authority. I lay my crown down at your feet and ask you to take the throne in my castle. You are my Lord. You are the King of my castle. Lead me, Lord. Teach me to live by the Spirit. Teach me to obey your voice. Cover me, Lord, protect me, provide for me Lord. Give me your faith, give me your courage. Send me out in the power of your name to destroy the works of the enemy in my castle and beyond.

Lord, I give you my heart today. Please come and fill my heart with your love by your Holy Spirit. Give me an undivided heart. Purify my heart, Lord. Wash through me and fill my heart with your desires. Forgive me, Lord, where I have given affection to things that should never have been in my heart. May I always turn my heart to the throne room and away from the world. May you be the greatest influence on my heart every day. I love you, Lord.

Lord, in your light we see light. I thank you that we have the mind of Christ. Give me more revelation about my thinking. Expose my blind spots, Lord. Show me when I am believing lies about you and about myself. Show me when I am thinking impure or unloving thoughts. Lord, give me your wisdom. Teach me your ways, Lord, and show me things I do not know.

Lord, I dedicate my body to you today. I am a temple for your Holy Spirit. My body was paid for by Jesus on the cross. Sin will no longer master me, as you are my master. Lord, lead me today, give me revelation to see when I am under attack and to act with wisdom at all times. Remind me that sin cannot rule over me, because you are on the throne of my castle. Above all else, may my mind, will and emotions guard my heart and may I turn to you for leadership, guidance, love and comfort. Amen

Decrees

I am speaking to sin. I come to you in the authority of Jesus Christ who lives in me and is greater than anything that is in the world. I resist you and stand firm in the faith of Christ. No weapon you use against me will prosper. I condemn any word of accusation sent against me. I have the victory in this battle because I am in Christ, who is victorious in all things. You are a defeated enemy because Jesus nailed you to the cross and made a public spectacle of you. I command you to leave now and never to return. In the name of Jesus.

Lord, I will ruthlessly pursue the truth. I will speak the truth about you and about myself. I refuse to believe the lies the enemy has told me. I will renew my mind with your word and use the sword of the spirit, which is the word of God, to demolish ungodly arguments and pretensions that have set themselves up in my castle in opposition to the knowledge of God. I will take every ungodly thought captive and throw it down at the cross to make it obedient to you. In the name of Jesus.

I will walk with you in complete freedom, for I seek to follow your every command.

When I stand before kings, I will tell them the truth and will never be ashamed.

My passion and delight is in your word, for I love what you say to me!

I long for more revelation of your truth, for I love the light of your word as I meditate on your decrees.

Amen.

ABOUT THE AUTHOR

Peter Jones is the ministry director for Europe and the Middle East for Alpha International. He previously worked as a detached youth worker with gangs in the UK and ran Alpha in prisons for seven years. He currently oversees Alpha in prisons globally. He has a master's degree in criminology and criminal justice. Peter lives in Oxford UK, is married to Titilola from Nigeria, and has two grown children.

www.kingofthecastle.net

Visit www.kingofthecastle.net for more information, free downloads, blog and communities to join.

Printed in Great Britain
by Amazon